SCOTTISH LANDSCAPES

By Alan and Moira McKirdy

Illustrated by Craig Ellery

Edinburgh : The Stationery Office

Scottish Natural Heritage

National Museums of Scotland

SCOTLAND – A LAND OF CONTRASTS

Mountains and moorlands, cities and coasts – Scotland has them all. Each part of the country has its own unique character. But what makes Scotland so special? Why do so many visitors come to Scotland each year? Is it for the Highland hospitality or the breathtaking view from the top of Ben Lomond? It is probably a bit of both!

Britain is a crowded island. Most people live in towns and cities, so remote and rugged areas, such as the Highlands of Scotland, have a special appeal. In fact, the landscape is the basis for one of Scotland's most important industries – tourism.

Wildlife is an important part of the landscape. Ospreys and oystercatchers, pine forests and peat bogs all contribute to the special character of the land. Although you might expect to find the rarer plants and animals in remote Highland glens, city streets are sometimes just as good a place for spotting wildlife.

Describe the landscape you can see from your bedroom window. Describe another very different view of a Scottish landscape. What are the main differences?

ROCKS AND LANDSCAPES

The look of the landscape owes a great deal to the rocks beneath our feet. Granites, lavas and other rocks which have formed from molten rock or magma from deep within the Earth's crust, build many of Scotland's highest peaks and mountain areas. The flatter, gently rolling parts of lowland Scotland have softer rocks underneath. These rocks, called sandstones and shales, are more easily worn away. So the rocks determine the nature of the landscape, which in turn influences the kind of plants and animals that live there.

Scotland's landscape has taken over three thousand million years to become what we see today. During that time, Scotland's climate has changed from being as hot as the Sahara desert to the deep freeze of the Ice Age. These events have all left their mark on the landscape.

The most productive farmland is to be found on the east coast, whilst the more mountainous landscapes of the west coast are more suited to sheep farming. The rocks not only influence the kind of plants and animals we find in every part of the countryside, but also shape the lives of everyone who lives there.

Orkney Islands

Flow Country

St. Kilda

Loch Garten

Deeside

Perthshire

Holyrood Park

Do you know what flora, fauna and habitat mean? If not, look them up. Answers on page 40. Now match these plants and animals to particular landscapes or locations throughout Scotland. You may have to read the whole book to answer these questions.

- sphagnum moss
- puffin
- osprey
- Scottish primrose
- Scots pine
- sticky catchfly
- wildcat

Scotland's mountains are famous the world over. The Scottish peaks are not as high as the Alps or Himalayas, but because they are easily reached from the towns and cities, most are popular with hillwalkers and mountaineers. Ben Nevis, near Fort William, the Cuillin on Skye and the Cairngorms are three of Scotland's highest and best known mountain areas. These wild and rugged places have inspired poets and painters.

Peaks over 3,000 feet (or 914 m) are called "Munros". These are named after Sir Hugh Munro (1856 – 1919) who was a keen mountaineer. There are 277 Munros in Scotland and many people have great fun trying to climb them. Sir Hugh managed to climb all of them except the *Inaccessible Pinnacle* on Skye, although he tried several times. Climbing Munros is now a popular pastime. This is nicknamed "Munro-bagging".

THE INACCESSIBLE PINNACLE

Find out where your nearest Munro is located. An atlas, or even better, an Ordnance Survey map will help you find the answer. Do not rush off and climb it on your own as some Munros are dangerous places, even for experienced climbers.

A Landscape Before People

For two million years, great sheets of ice and snow covered Scotland. This was the Ice Age. These ice sheets wore away the rocks and shaped the landscape of Scotland. It was only around 10,000 years ago that the ice melted. The *Great Wood of Caledon*, a vast area of Scots Pine trees, then grew on the higher land. Wolves and wild boar roamed this forest, sharing the landscape with brown bears, lynx and elk. The Romans occupied much of the southern part of Scotland, but they cared little for the wooded Highlands to the north. Later, the Vikings came from Norway. They cut down parts of the Great Wood to make their longboats. The wildlife was gradually driven out by these changes. Brown bears died out in Scotland around a thousand years ago and the last wolf was killed in 1743 in Inverness-shire.

The Highland clan chiefs cut down many of the trees on their lands to sell the wood and, during the two world wars, more trees were felled to make railway sleepers and telegraph poles. All that now remains of the once mighty wood are a few small areas, such as in the Cairngorms, Rannoch Moor and Glen Affric.

The Scots pine has not been able to grow again in great numbers, mainly because there are too many deer and sheep nibbling at any seedlings that appear. However, at Mar Lodge in the Cairngorms, deer and sheep have been kept out by fences, so the seedlings are being allowed to grow into trees. The Great Wood of Caledon may rise again!

Draw a picture of what your area ago. would have looked like Scots pine and birch grew in the lowlands remember that oak and buildings, roads or fields. Remember, while there were no hills, there were no and there were

MOORLANDS

Below the jagged peaks and broad plateaux of the mountains lies the moorland. Much of this land was once covered by trees, but now, a thick carpet of heather, bracken and rough grassland has spread across the land. In many areas, the heather is set on fire each year, as this encourages better growth of young plants next season. Drastic action, you may think, but this has been done in some areas for over 3,000 years – so it must work.

The heather moorland is home to many different types of birds, for example the red grouse. Many Highland landowners allow visitors to come on to their moorland to shoot these birds. People come from abroad for this type of sport.

Moorland covers the greater part of Scotland. It is an area that we do not know quite so well as the impressive mountain ranges or the coastal areas, as it sometimes appears flat, featureless and boggy underfoot. Not necessarily the kind of place you would choose for a walk.

The Scots word for moorland is "muir". Look up your map and find the nearest muir to where you live. What is this area used for?

THE "FLOW COUNTRY"

Large areas of Caithness and Sutherland are covered by a thick blanket of "bog". This is called the "Flow Country". The land here is made up of sphagnum moss, peat and areas of water. At first sight, it looks barren, as there are no trees to be seen. If you look and listen carefully, you will find it is an exciting place for wildlife.

The most spectacular bog plants are those that trap and eat insects – for example the sundews. The scent of bog myrtle, the buzz of dragonfly wings and the songs of skylarks and meadow pipits are some of the common smells and sounds of the "Flow Country". Even the majestic red deer can be found bathing in some of the deep water pools. These peaty pools are called *dubh lochain*, which means "small black loch" in Gaelic.

Because it is so difficult to grow crops or build houses or roads on the water-logged peat, these areas have remained almost unchanged for thousands of years. Look across this landscape and the view you see will be little different to that seen by people in the Bronze Age, almost two thousand years ago. Many changes have taken place in other parts of the landscape during this time. The forests of Scots pine have been cut down and towns and cities have been built, but the blanket bog of the "Flow Country" has altered little.

For centuries, peat has been used as a fuel for the fire. Blocks of peat are cut using a special spade and then stacked during the summer months to dry. As winter approaches, the dried peat is gathered and stored for burning during the winter.

Peat is also used to make garden compost. In recent years, large areas of the "Flow Country" and other boglands in the lowlands of Scotland have been dug up and destroyed. You can help to stop this destruction if you use compost made from other materials.

When you next visit a garden centre, see how many brands of compost you can find that do not contain any peat.

What are the other options?

Answer on page 40.

LOCHS AND RIVERS

There are over 30,000 freshwater lochs in Scotland, most containing a variety of fish and other wildlife, such as otters and water-lilies. Lochs are popular places where people go to admire the scenery, catch fish and sail their boats. Loch Ness holds more water than all the lakes in England and Wales put together...and perhaps a few monsters besides! Loch Lomond is the biggest and Loch Morar is the deepest loch in Britain.

There are lots of rivers and burns in Scotland too – over 5,000 of them. The River Tay is Scotland's biggest river. It rises as a tiny burn near Beinn Laoigh and flows across Perthshire to the sea. There are lots of salmon in the River Tay and many people catch and sell these fish. A salmon lives in the sea for part of its life. It returns to the river where it was born to breed. On its journey upstream, it must pass many hazards, such as waterfalls and dams. At Faskally Dam, at Pitlochry, the fish pass through a special channel to the other side of the dam. Visitors can visit a viewing chamber from where they can see the fish swim upstream.

Freshwater from a burn or loch may look clean, but is it? Factories, farms and even homes produce chemicals which may cause water pollution. These poisons can be absorbed by plants, through their roots and stems, and this will do them harm. You can show how easily plants can absorb dirty water by using coloured water in your experiment. After only a few hours, the flower and stem of the celery become coloured.

Put celery and a white flower in coloured water (e.g. food colouring)

What happens after a few hours?

The River Tay is also famous for freshwater pearls, which occasionally form inside a type of shellfish, called a *mussel*. Because of pollution and too many people trying to catch them, they are now very rare.

COASTS AND SEASCAPES

The coastline of Scotland is almost 12,000 kilometres long. If you flew that distance in a straight line westwards from Scotland, you would end up in California. If you look at a map of the west coast, you will see why the coast is so long. It twists and turns, forming sealochs and headlands, and there are also many islands. This is a landscape of constant changes. The tides come in and out twice a day. The waves break on the shore, gently in fine weather and as huge rollers during winter storms.

Most of our coastline is rocky. Some cliffs are higher than the tallest buildings in Scotland and plunge straight into the sea. Only the hardiest seabirds and sealife can survive in these conditions. These steep cliffs are normally found on the west coast and are home to seabirds such as kittiwakes, puffins and arctic terns.

The east coast is very different. There are more sandy beaches and shingle banks. In broad inlets, called estuaries, areas of mud and sand have collected around the shoreline. These mudflats are home to many different types of worm and other soft-bodied animals, which are a rich source of food for many wading birds, such as oystercatchers and curlews. At sea, seals, dolphins and porpoises feed on the rich supply of fish.

The estuaries of the Forth and Tay are also important areas for industry, such as shipping and refining oil, so careful planning is needed to make sure that this valuable landscape remains unspoilt.

The fish in the sea around the coasts feed on minute creatures called plankton. The fish are then eaten by dolphins. This is called a food chain.
Can you make up another food chain?
Answers on page 40.

Plankton → Fish

Dolphin

ISLANDS OF SCOTLAND

There are hundreds of islands around the coastline of Scotland – about 800 in fact and that is only counting those where grass or other plants grow. No one has ever counted the smaller rocky islands, known as *skerries*. There must be thousands of those.

St. Kilda is one of the most remote island groups. It lies about 190 kilometres west of the Scottish mainland, surrounded by the Atlantic Ocean. People lived in this remote place for many centuries. Crops were difficult to grow, but there was a plentiful supply of fish. Seabirds, such as gannets and puffins, nested on the very steep cliffs. The islanders risked their lives to catch them and collect their eggs. Children were taught to climb cliffs as soon as they were able, so that they could help with this task. The people who lived on St. Kilda had to be very hardy as the weather was often cold and wet. The men met every morning to decide on the work to be done that day.

Rothesay on the **Island of Bute** is still a popular place to visit. During the Glasgow Fair holiday, the paddle steamer *Waverley* took many passengers on the trip "doon the watter". Now, many of the islands of Scotland are visited by thousands of tourists from all over the world every summer.

Ailsa Craig is a well-known landmark off the coast of Ayrshire. It is called Paddy's Milestone, because it is half-way between Scotland and Ireland. In years gone by, curling stones were made from the granite rock of Ailsa Craig.

Find the names of TEN Scottish islands. (Answers on page 40.)

```
A R R Q R X F N G M C O
O I S L E W I S F W O R
J K L P R B U T O P D K
E U D S C S S K Y E B N
M O P H A K F I O X A E
Y Z X E L C O L S R P Y
T B U T E E R D R G W N
N Q W L T U K A H V F T
S U T A D L Z F I N K H
L I O N A D B Z C G R M
P U R D V A M E A O L Q
U B M R C O A G L P H E
```

LANDSCAPE-HOPPING

A game for 1–4 players (need dice and counters). Time how long it takes to visit Scotland's landscapes. Game begins in Edinburgh. Finishes in Glasgow.

12 Travel to Flow Country – throw a 2 to catch the ferry

13 Flow Country

14 Stuck in a bog – throw a 3 to get out!

11 Have another throw

18

17 Travel to Skye

Spot wild flowers on the Machair – miss a turn

15 Travel to Loch Ness

Ski down the mountain – have another turn

8

9 Travel to Aberdeen

10 Catch a flight to Orkney to birdwatch on the seacliffs

19 Travel to Bute – sail "doon the watter"

16 Spot Nessie – have 2 throws

7 Travel to the Cairngorms

Travel to

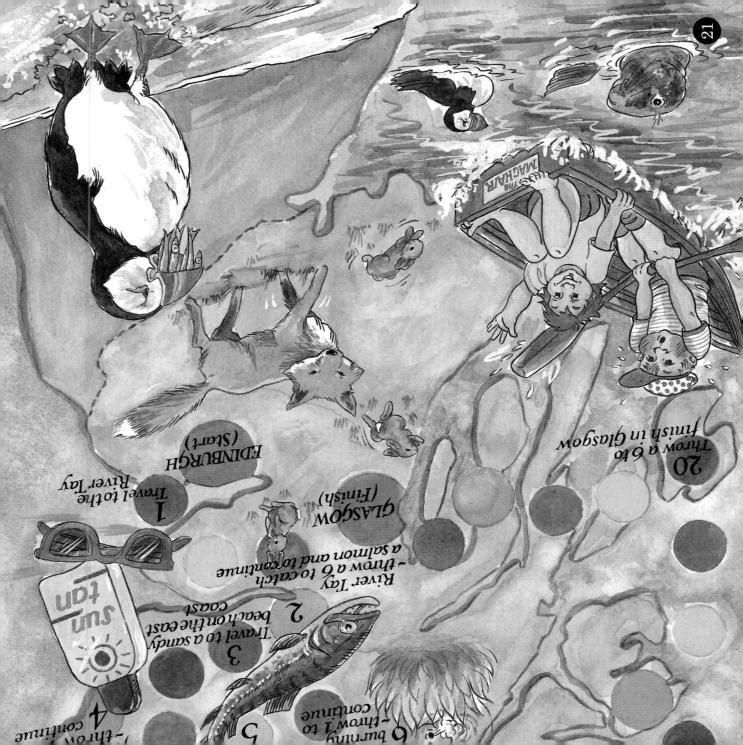

MACHAIR

Along the Atlantic coast of the Western Isles and along other stretches of coast in northern Scotland, there is a very special landscape called machair. In Gaelic, this means "the low-lying meadow near the sands of the shore". In summer, it is a blaze of colour with many types of wild flowers, insects and birds. This thin strip of land beside the sea is farmed by people, called crofters, in a way that has changed little for hundreds of years. They use few chemicals to fertilise the land, so this helps wildlife to flourish. Instead, seaweed is sometimes ploughed into the ground. This acts as a natural fertiliser and helps their crops, such as potatoes, to grow. Crofters often have other jobs, such as postmen, fishermen or community workers, as the areas of land they tend are small.

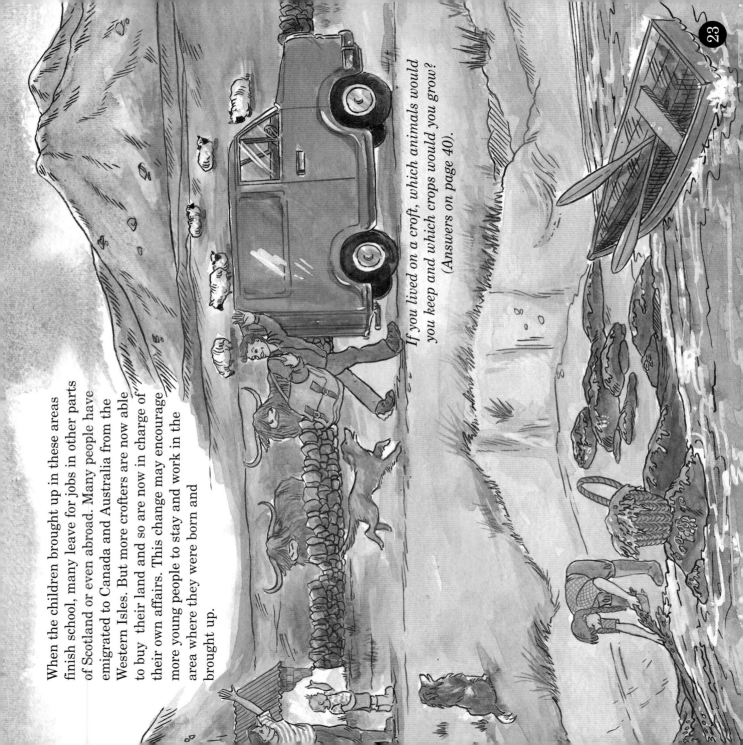

When the children brought up in these areas finish school, many leave for jobs in other parts of Scotland or even abroad. Many people have emigrated to Canada and Australia from the Western Isles. But more crofters are now able to buy their land and so are now in charge of their own affairs. This change may encourage more young people to stay and work in the area where they were born and brought up.

If you lived on a croft, which animals would you keep and which crops would you grow? (Answers on page 40).

CITYSCAPES

Most of the population live in towns and cities. This is a landscape built by people, for people. Many of our towns and cities were built many years ago, using local materials. The red sandstone tenements of Glasgow and the grey granite terraced houses of Aberdeen are an important part of the character of these great cities. Edinburgh Castle and the grand houses of Edinburgh's New Town create a cityscape which is every bit as impressive as the wild, undeveloped Highland landscapes.

People are an important part of the city landscape. There is great hustle and bustle as everyone rushes to where they want to go – in cars, buses or on foot. Horns toot, engines roar, an aeroplane flies overhead – the noise can be deafening.

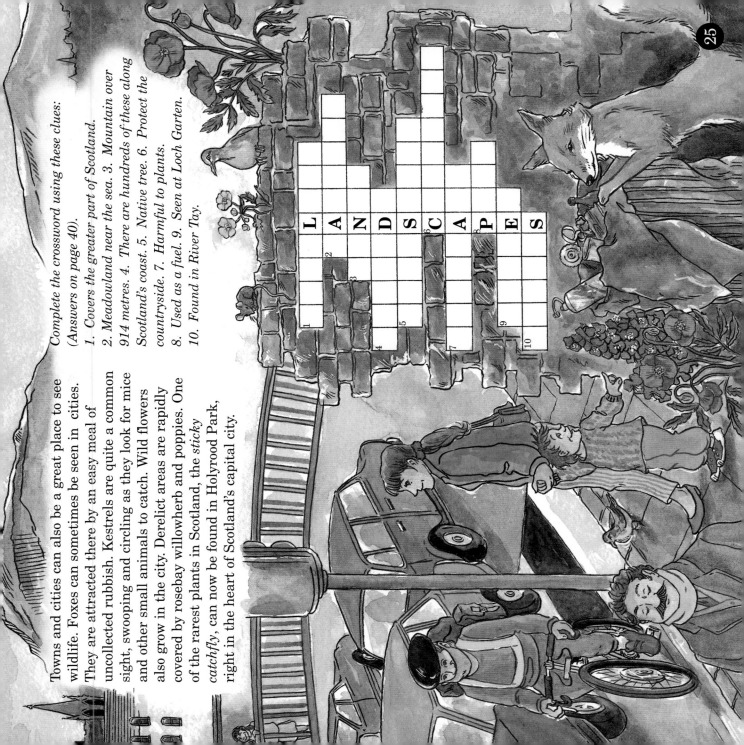

Towns and cities can also be a great place to see wildlife. Foxes can sometimes be seen in cities. They are attracted there by an easy meal of uncollected rubbish. Kestrels are quite a common sight, swooping and circling as they look for mice and other small animals to catch. Wild flowers also grow in the city. Derelict areas are rapidly covered by rosebay willowherb and poppies. One of the rarest plants in Scotland, the sticky *catchfly*, can now be found in Holyrood Park, right in the heart of Scotland's capital city.

Complete the crossword using these clues: (Answers on page 40).

1. Covers the greater part of Scotland.
2. Meadowland near the sea. 3. Mountain over 914 metres. 4. There are hundreds of these along Scotland's coast. 5. Native tree. 6. Protect the countryside. 7. Harmful to plants.
8. Used as a fuel. 9. Seen at Loch Garten.
10. Found in River Tay.

INDUSTRIAL LANDSCAPES

The way Scots earned their living in the past has also left its mark on the landscape. For the last few hundred years, coal has been mined and oil refined in Scotland. The rock and soil left over from coal mining were piled into great heaps, called *bings*. They are a familiar part of the landscape in central Scotland, particularly around Glasgow and south of Edinburgh. In West Lothian, there are many great piles of red shale. This is a reminder of the industry that extracted oil from oilshale.

Canals were once the main way of transporting goods around the country. Most are now disused and have become overgrown with weeds. Some industrial areas are badly polluted with chemicals but, amazingly, some plants, such as orchids and rare mosses, manage to grow in these places.

Industrial landscapes are changing as new developments come along. The foundations of a shopping centre in Edinburgh used the material from a nearby shale bing. Reusing or recycling materials for building, instead of digging out new deposits of sand, gravel and rock is another way of saving the environment.

Some developments, such as the petrochemical plant at Grangemouth, can be seen for miles and are a very prominent part of the landscape – especially at night with the gas flares ablaze. The air released from some factories may contain poisonous gases, such as sulphur dioxide. This forms an acid when mixed with water and may fall as *acid rain* across the countryside. Acid rain is harmful to plants and animals.

- *what other types of recycling do you know about?*
- *show the effect of acid rain on plants*
  - take three plant cuttings in small pots.
  - stand in saucers containing
    - (A) *water*
    - (B) *weak vinegar solution*
    - (C) *strong vinegar solution*

Keep watering with their own mixture A, B or C and note what happens. See page 40.

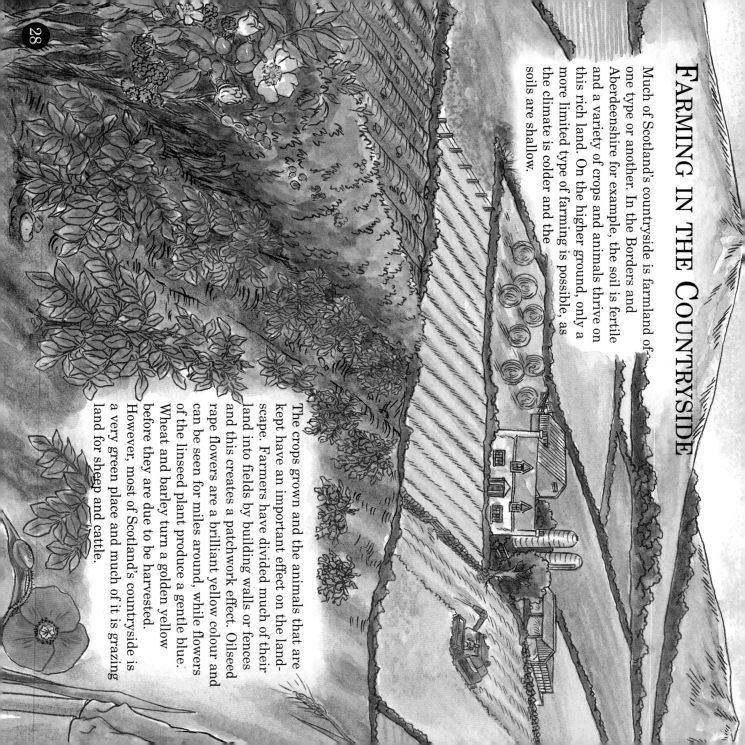

FARMING IN THE COUNTRYSIDE

Much of Scotland's countryside is farmland of one type or another. In the Borders and Aberdeenshire for example, the soil is fertile and a variety of crops and animals thrive on this rich land. On the higher ground, only a more limited type of farming is possible, as the climate is colder and the soils are shallow.

The crops grown and the animals that are kept have an important effect on the landscape. Farmers have divided much of their land into fields by building walls or fences and this creates a patchwork effect. Oilseed rape flowers are a brilliant yellow colour and can be seen for miles around, while flowers of the linseed plant produce a gentle blue. Wheat and barley turn a golden yellow before they are due to be harvested. However, most of Scotland's countryside is a very green place and much of it is grazing land for sheep and cattle.

Farmers have an important job to do in looking after wildlife. Farming has changed in recent years to make greater use of the land available. Fields have been enlarged by the cutting down of hedgerows, thereby reducing wildlife habitats. Storage of crops is now in modern buildings rather than in small wooden barns. The number of barn owls and bats has decreased as a result. We must be careful to balance our need for food with our love of wildlife and wild land.

Make your own soil indicator. Soils can be acid, neutral or alkaline. You can test the soils in your area if you make your own soil indicator. The best material to use is red cabbage, but you can also try rose petals or geranium flowers. Chop up $\frac{1}{4}$ of a small red cabbage. Place in 200 ml of water in a small saucepan and heat until boiling. Boil for about 5 minutes. Strain off the cabbage and collect the coloured liquid. This is your indicator. Test whether your indicator works:

1. Water.
2. Bicarbonate of soda solution.
3. Lemon juice.

Place a teaspoonful of the test liquids on a white plate. Add $\frac{1}{2}$ teaspoon of indicator.

Now take a soil sample and mix with water. Allow to settle out. Test the liquid.

What type of soil do you have?

FLORA...

Some **Scots pines** are over 400 years old. They were seedlings when James VI was King of Scotland! At one time, Scots pine covered much of the Highlands – the Great Wood of Caledon. Only small patches of this wood now remain.

The **Sticky catchfly** is a rare plant indeed, found only in a few places in Scotland. Plants grown from local seeds have been planted in Holyrood Park.

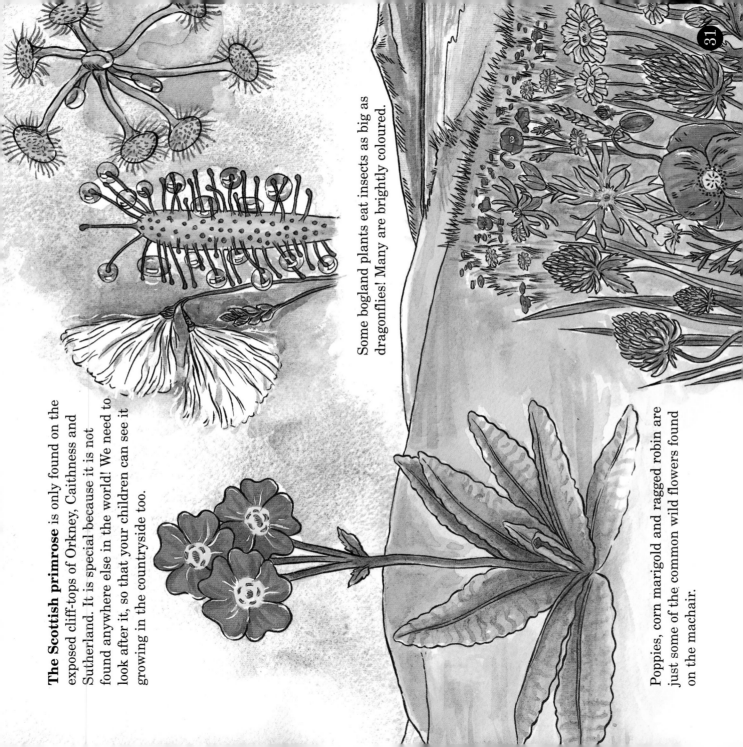

The Scottish primrose is only found on the exposed cliff-tops of Orkney, Caithness and Sutherland. It is special because it is not found anywhere else in the world! We need to look after it, so that your children can see it growing in the countryside too.

Some bogland plants eat insects as big as dragonflies! Many are brightly coloured.

Poppies, corn marigold and ragged robin are just some of the common wild flowers found on the machair.

...AND FAUNA

Ospreys were a common sight at one time, but they were hunted and their eggs stolen over a long period so they almost became extinct in Scotland. Recently, chicks have been successfully hatched at Loch Garten, near Aviemore, and the public are able to watch the nest or eyrie from a special viewing area.

Pine martens are nocturnal. They tend to hunt at night, so you are unlikely to see one when you are out in the countryside. They live mainly in wooded areas. They hunt small birds and mammals and will also eat eggs. You can imagine that they are not very popular with farmers.

Red deer are a wonderful sight grazing quietly by the roadside or picking their way gracefully across the hill. In the breeding season, the males fight each other, locking antlers and bellowing loudly.

The **golden eagle** is a majestic sight. Its wings, stretched out in flight, are as wide as a man is tall – about two metres. It nests on cliff ledges in remote mountain areas and glides effortlessly over the Highland glens in search of its prey.

Although once found throughout Britain, the **wildcat** is now found only in the Highlands.

The **mountain hare's** coat changes with the seasons. During the winter, the coat changes to white to blend in with the snow. Its natural enemies, such as the golden eagle, cannot easily see it. Some hares moult, or change their coats, as many as three times during the year.

CHANGING SEASONS

The countryside changes with the seasons. As temperatures rise in the **spring**, the countryside begins to come to life. Snow melts on all but the highest ground and animals that have been asleep for winter come out of hibernation. Plants also awake from their dormant state and new shoots begin to appear. This is the time when visitors start to walk in the hills and fish the burns and lochs.

The countryside is at its most colourful during the **summer**. Wild flowers bloom and the heather spreads a beautiful purple carpet across the hills. During the school holiday period especially, the hills and beaches, towns and cities become a haven for visitors.

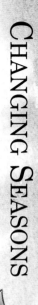

Have you got a favourite view? It could be the view from your bedroom window or from the local park. Draw a series of pictures of your favourite view, noting the main changes which take place throughout the year.

34

Then, as suddenly as this invasion of people started, the visitors melt away - until next spring. The flowers fade, the **autumn** rain falls and then the first frosts come. With the harvest gathered from the fields and the visitors long gone, the countryside and all who live there prepare for another long winter.

In **winter**, the trees are bare and the hills may be snow-covered. The weather is often cold, with sharp frosts and long, dark nights. Braemar, on Deeside, is often the coldest place in Britain and temperatures recorded here are often lower than those in Moscow.

If you do not know what *hibernation* means, look it up! The answer is given on Page 40.

ENJOYING THE COUNTRYSIDE

There is so much to do in the countryside. Climbing mountains, walking the hills or just lazing around by the seaside. As most of us live in towns and cities, it is great to get away from the crowds and enjoy the peace and quiet of the countryside. But even the most remote spots, like the high tops of Cairngorm, can be quite busy with skiers during the winter months and with hillwalkers during the rest of the year.

Many people come to Scotland to enjoy the wonderful scenery. Visitors stay in hotels and guesthouses. They buy souvenirs to take back home and lots of people have jobs looking after these tourists. As the countryside is Scotland's most precious resource, we must look after it to make sure that it stays unspoiled.

ACTIVITY

Design a poster to attract tourists to Scotland. Include a variety of different scenes from around Scotland. This book should give you some good ideas.

Pencils and Brushes

One thing that can definitely spoil your day in the countryside is the dreaded midge! Midges are little insects about the size of the head of a pin and they fly about in swarms. Bare flesh, such as arms and legs, are a tempting meal that they find hard to resist. Many ways of warding off the midge have been tried over the years, but none have worked. So if you are out walking in the Highlands, just keep an eye out for them - because they will be watching you!

PROTECTING THE COUNTRYSIDE

The landscape is Scotland's most important asset. We must make sure that it stays that way. One way to protect the countryside is to choose special places and then ensure that houses, roads, quarries or other types of development are not allowed to spoil these areas. Land can be special because of its wildlife or beautiful scenery or because interesting rocks have been found there. *Scottish Natural Heritage* helps the landowners to look after these special areas. This is called *conservation* and more and more people now realise how important it is to look after the countryside. In recent years, farmers have ripped out many hedgerows, drained areas of wetland and used chemicals to make crops grow faster. Unfortunately, this has damaged the countryside in the process. However, things are changing. Many farmers are now more conservation-friendly. Payments can be made to them when they leave areas of rough grass to encourage wild flowers to grow or when they establish new areas of woodland.

There are now many groups that are interested in looking after the countryside, such as the *Royal Society for the Protection of Birds* or the *Scottish Wildlife Trust*. By joining, you can help to conserve your natural heritage of birds, bogs or woodland. Why not get your feet wet making a new pond or your hands dirty rebuilding a drystane dyke? You will find the addresses of these groups on page 40.

There are so many things to do these days. Watching the television and playing computer games can be great fun, but being out in the fresh air takes a bit of beating.

If you would like to join in with these types of activities, why not join the RSPB or the *Scottish Wildlife Trust.*

FOREST WALK

SCOTTISH BORDERS COUNCIL

INFORMATION SERVICES

SCOTTISH WILDLIFE TRUST

R.S.P.B.

PLACES TO VISIT AND ANSWERS

Places to Visit

- **Knockan Crag Visitor Centre**, near Ullapool
- **Beinn Eighe National Nature Reserve**, Highland
- **Orcadian Stone Company Visitor Centre**, Golspie
- **The Parallel Roads of Glen Roy National Nature Reserve**, near Fort William
- **Glen Coe**, near Ballachulish
- **Creag Meagaidh National Nature Reserve**, near Loch Laggan
- **St. Cyrus National Nature Reserve**
- **Ben Lawers National Nature Reserve**, Perthshire
- **Kinnoull Hill Forestry Trail**, near Perth
- **Loch Leven**, near Kinross
- **Falls of Clyde**, near Lanark
- **Loch Lomond Country Park**
- **Pentlands Country Park**, near Edinburgh
- **Holyrood Park**, Edinburgh
- **Vogrie Country Park**, near Pathhead

Answers

Pages 4/5: Flora = the plants which grow in a particular area. Fauna = the animals which live in a particular area. Habitat = the place where a particular animal or plant lives.

1. Sphagnum moss - Flow Country
2. Puffin - St. Kilda
3. Osprey - Loch Garten
4. Scottish primrose - Orkney
5. Scots pine - Deeside
6. Sticky catchfly - Holyrood Park
7. Wildcat - Perthshire

Pages 12/13: Composted tree bark, cocoa shells and compost made from garden waste.

Pages 16/17: Seaweed → periwinkle → mussel → starfish, dead and rotting organisms → crab → man.

Pages 18/19: Island Wordsearch

A	R	R	Q	R	X	F	N	G	M	C	O
O	I	S	L	E	W	I	S	F	W	O	R
J	K	L	P	R	B	U	T	O	P	D	K
E	U	D	S	C	S	K	Y	E	B	N	A
M	O	P	H	A	K	F	I	O	X	A	E
Y	Z	X	E	L	C	O	L	S	R	P	Y
T	B	U	F	E	E	R	D	R	G	W	N
N	Q	W	L	T	U	K	H	V	F	T	
S	U	T	A	D	L	Z	F	I	N	K	H
L	T	O	N	A	D	B	Z	C	G	R	M
P	U	R	D	V	A	M	E	A	O	L	Q
U	B	M	R	C	O	A	G	L	P	H	E

Pages 22/23: Crops: potatoes, oats, grass for haymaking. Animals: Cheviot sheep, cattle.

Pages 24/25: Crossword

MOORLAND, MACHAIR, MUNRO, ISLANDS, SCOTS PINE, CONSERVE, ACID RAIN, PEAT, OSPREY, PEARLS

Pages 26/27: Plant A remains healthy, whilst Plant C dies quickly followed by Plant B. Acid rain can have a similar effect on trees and other plants.

Pages 28/29: Results: 1. neutral; 2. alkaline; 3. acid.

Pages 34/35: Hibernation means to sleep through the cold winter months.

Pages 38/39: Scottish Wildlife Trust, Cramond House, Cramond Glebe Road, Edinburgh EH4 6NS. Tel: 0131-312 7765.

Royal Society for the Protection of Birds, 17 Regent Terrace, Edinburgh EH7 5BN. Tel: 0131-557 3136.